ALSO IN MIND

THE ONE

CHANAKA
ARIYARATNA

POEMS

ALSO IN MIND

THE ONE

CHANAKA
ARIYARATNA

POEMS

LINKTR.EE/ARIYARATNA

Also in Mind Copyright © 2022 by P G S Chanaka Ariyaratna
All rights reserved.

Printed in Australia. No part of this publication may be reproduced, distributed, or transmitted in any form or by any means, including photocopying, recording, or other electronic or mechanical methods, without the prior written permission of the publisher, except in the case of brief quotations embodied in critical reviews and certain other non-commercial uses permitted by copyright law. For permission requests, contact chanaka.ariyaratna@gmail.com

First published May 2023
Published by P G S Chanaka Ariyaratna
Also In Mind – The One

ISBN 978-0-6458148-0-4

Copyright © P G S Chanaka Ariyaratna, 2023

Email: chanaka.ariyaratna@gmail.com

Phone: 0450911337 / +94777700337

linktr.ee/Ariyaratna

Illustrations and cover design by Chanaka Ariyaratna

ALSO IN MIND

FROM ALL MY MIND TO
ALL IN MY HEART

ALSO IN MIND

It is up to you
to

RECREATE

LOVE

FOREVER

MORE

ALSO IN MIND

CONTENTS

1
RECREATE
Fancy a Frisk?
page 10

2
LOVE
Blinding You & Binding Me
page 30

3
FOREVER
Forget Time
page 51

4
MORE
Becoming the Beyond
page 72

ALSO IN MIND

CHAPTER
I

RECREATE

Fancy A Frisk?

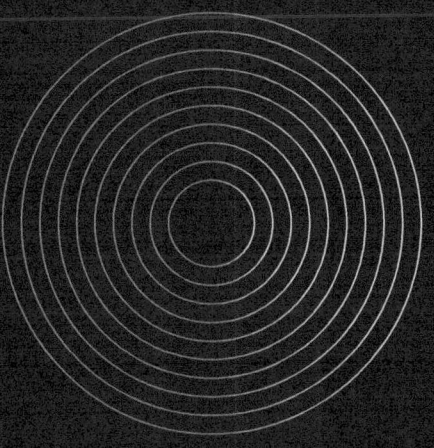

RECREATE
ALSO IN MIND

You are both
the Cause and the Calm
of my Storm

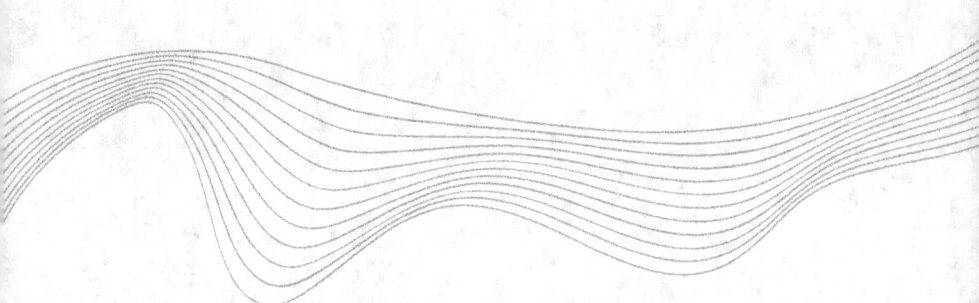

Storm

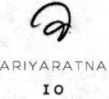

ARIYARATNA

RECREATE
ALSO IN MIND

In a world of people
who make you crazy and mad,
find the ones
who make you happy and glad,
cherish every moment
cherish every night,
be at your truest
be yourself, in spite

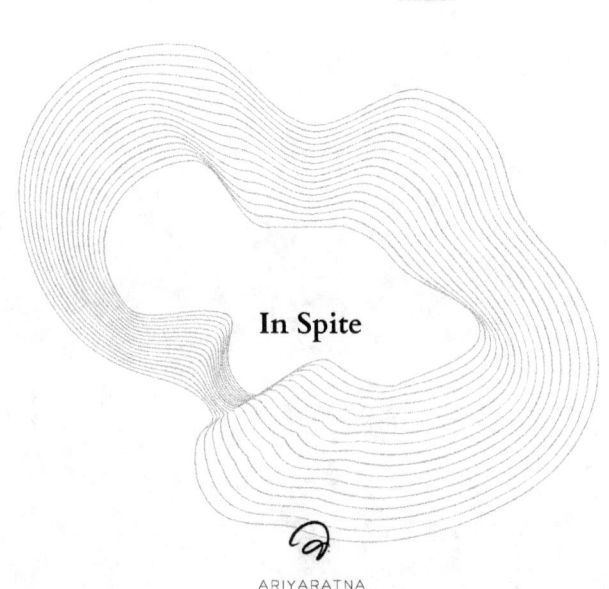

In Spite

ARIYARATNA

RECREATE
ALSO IN MIND

It looks like they took all the pieces
of my broken heart
and paved it all across Europe

Paved

ARIYARATNA

RECREATE
ALSO IN MIND

Armor Around me
Is not to protect me,
it's to make me heavy,
So you have enough time to run

Protect

ARIYARATNA

RECREATE
ALSO IN MIND

Heartthrob for Blooms
Adores the Moons
Heavy on the spoon
Not to fall in love too soon

Reminder

RECREATE
ALSO IN MIND

Fade me into the nights
Raise me into the mornings
Cease me in the days
Freeze me my stupid feelings
Jewel my thoughts Forget my ways
Jade all my meaning in this month of May

Jaded

Thought so much to write some lines
Thought so much to make them rhyme
Thought so much to create the flow
Thought so much about her glow
Thought so much to be so brave
Thought a bit too much, I forgot to Save

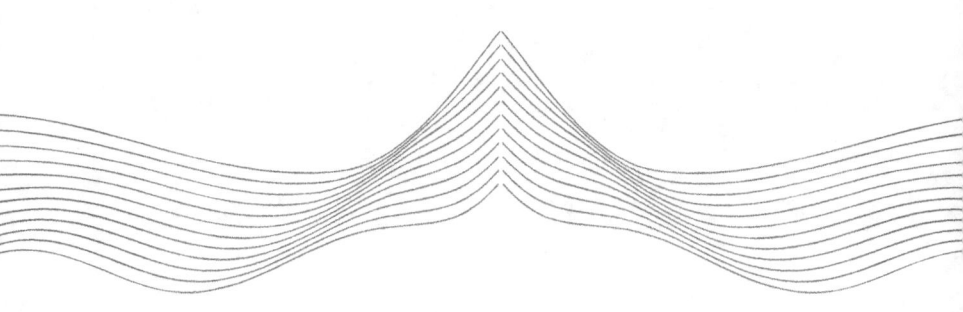

Forgot to Save

RECREATE
ALSO IN MIND

Lock up my body
Lock down my soul
Lock Away my desire
Lockout my gold
Lock in my love
Lock on my gaze
Lock everything to solve this craze

Locksmith

> RECREATE
> ALSO IN MIND

Tonight
Both the Sky and I feel the Gloom
Sad that we don't get to see the Moon

The Sky and I

ARIYARATNA

RECREATE
ALSO IN MIND

Would you Love me for all
Would you Love me for the falls
Would you Love me for the mistakes
Would you Love me for the cakes
Would you Love me for the fit
Would you Love me for the Hell of it

Me for The

RECREATE
ALSO IN MIND

Tell me to tell you,
What you need to hear
Touch me to touch you,
So I can take away your fear
Let me to let you,
Love endlessly my dear
Find me to find you
So you can end up here

Me to You

ARIYARATNA

RECREATE
ALSO IN MIND

I think I have been looking for
The wrong kind of person,
Someone who keeps, cherishes and reasons,
When I feel it should really be easy to tango,
Someone with anger, that can easily let go,
For then its done, we start a new,
Everyday fresh with no Emotional curfew

Emotional Curfew

ARIYARATNA

RECREATE
ALSO IN MIND

I told her she's not my type
I told her I'm not for play
I told her I'v done this hype
I told her to stay away
I told her that I can't love
That none of it matters anyway
I told her what I should have
Told myself every night & everyday

The Telling Story

ARIYARATNA

RECREATE
ALSO IN MIND

If she knew, I wouldn't Love
If she saw, I couldn't Love
If she said, I shouldn't Love
Only If She'd... Love

If She

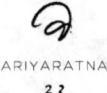

ARIYARATNA

RECREATE
ALSO IN MIND

Why don't you take your time
Sort things out make it rhyme
Think about it reconsider
Reinvent and Reinvigor
Leave and give your sorrows a rest
Meet me right outside your Nest
Be happy be mine
Be loved always, not sometimes

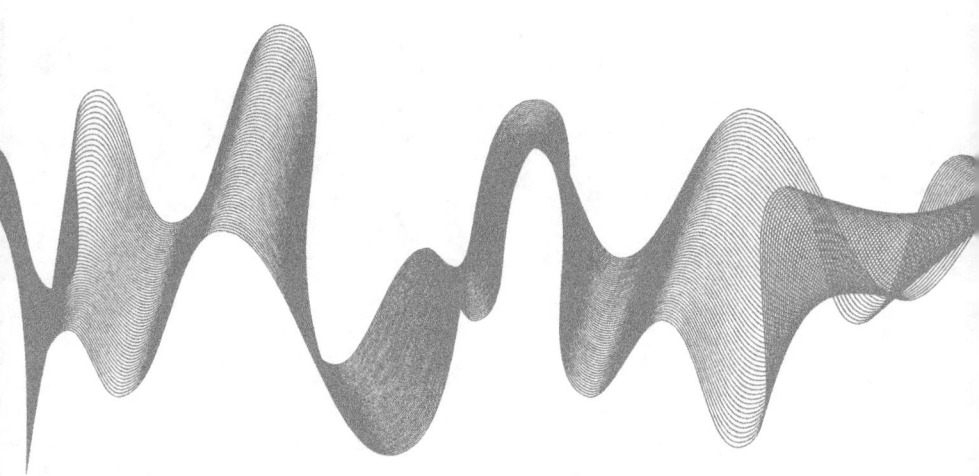

Reinvent

RECREATE
ALSO IN MIND

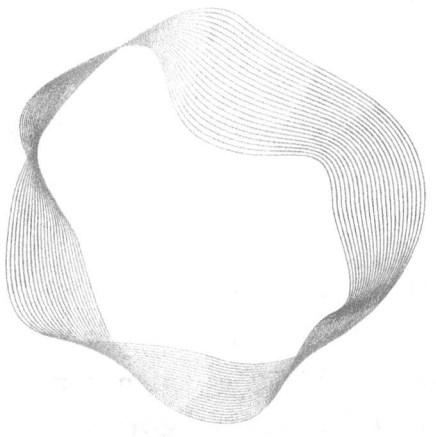

I have enough to fill my Mind
So that I have the courage to find
The heart you made Blind
A someone who is a bit more Kind

Engage

RECREATE
ALSO IN MIND

What more do you want me to do
I have done enough and more for you
Sleepless nights, goddamn mornings
You could have told me, given me warnings
You thought all will be fine and bright
Just let me be, just forget it, alright

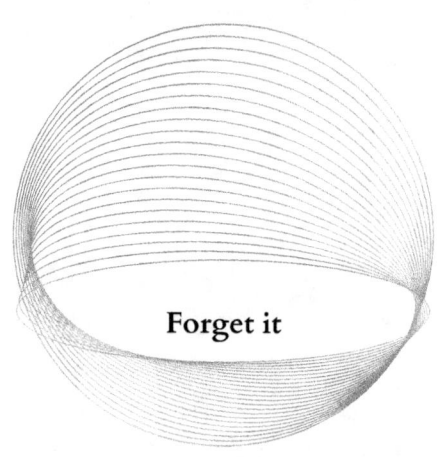

Forget it

ARIYARATNA

I think miss you
Which I should not
I think we should
Talk before you are lost
I think we would
Both be happy
I think we should
Cause it's just whacky

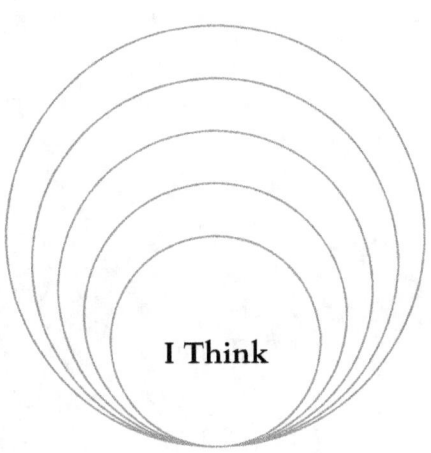

ARIYARATNA

RECREATE
ALSO IN MIND

I would want to win her over
I would totally be able to
I would surely hurt her
I wouldn't want her blue
I rather keep her safe
From my soul so dark
Even if it means no chafe
and even after Sparks

Chafe

ALSO IN MIND

CHAPTER
2

LOVE

Blinding You & Binding Me

LOVE
ALSO IN MIND

Hearts and Cookies are similar
You should not break or share them

Love of Cookie

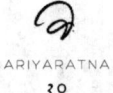

ARIYARATNA

LOVE
ALSO IN MIND

Your Perfume was all over me.
How can I be all over you

Perfume

ARIYARATNA

LOVE
ALSO IN MIND

In his dreams
as he passed her by
he whispered
"I have missed…you so much"

Stammer

ARIYARATNA

LOVE
ALSO IN MIND

I have late-night conversations with the Moon,
she tells me how she missed
Me during dusk,

I tell her how I missed her during noon

She Tells

ARIYARATNA

LOVE
ALSO IN MIND

Love not spoken of is the truest
Hearts broken are the strongest
Calls not dialed are the longest
Hugs not felt are the warmest

2 Min

ARIYARATNA

LOVE
ALSO IN MIND

If only giving up on you
Was as easy as falling for you

Liberty Less

ARIYARATNA

LOVE
ALSO IN MIND

She and I have been quite quiet
My heart, However
Has been Lovesick Loud

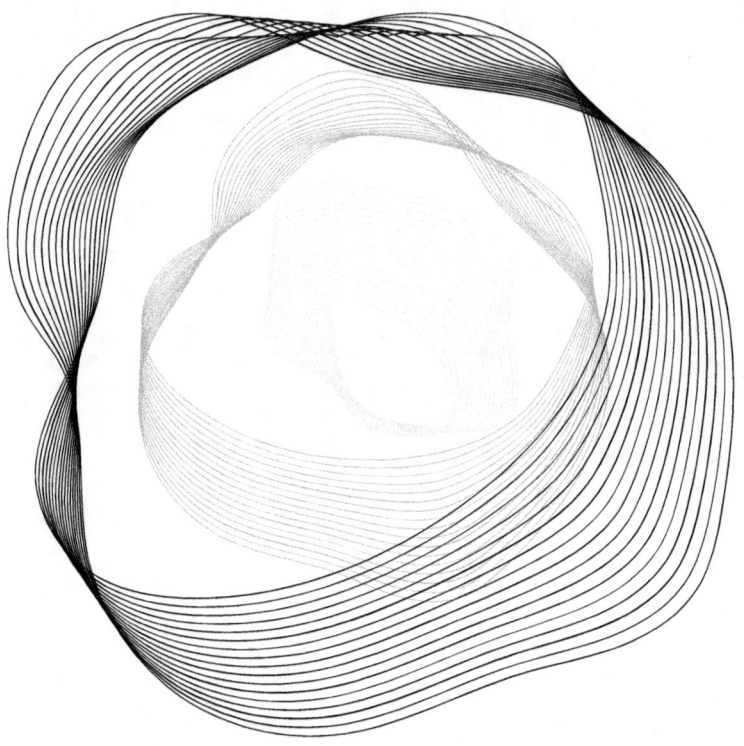

Loud

ARIYARATNA

LOVE
ALSO IN MIND

Sometimes hearts break
Sometimes hearts are on breaks
Sometimes hearts brake
And sometimes brakes break

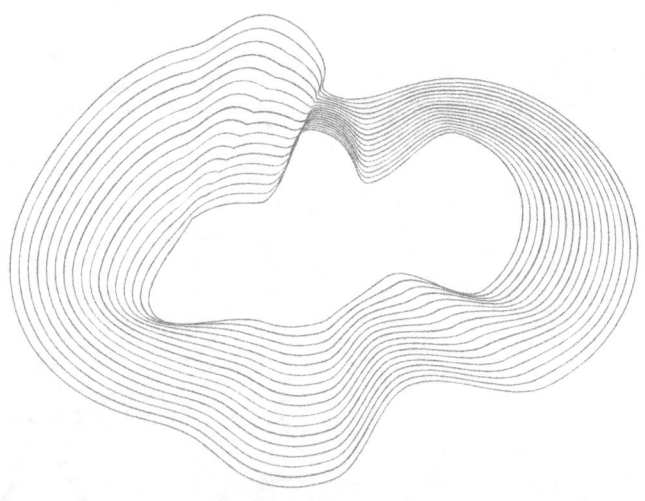

Breaking Brakes

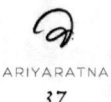

ARIYARATNA

LOVE
ALSO IN MIND

I Hate this world cause it didn't let me love her
The way she was meant to be loved

While I tried changing the World
She tried changing her mind

I just couldn't enough
She could just enough

Hate the World

ARIYARATNA

LOVE
ALSO IN MIND

So you've heard of broken hearts with
Pieces to fix,
but now mines more like powder too
Fine to mix

Heart Powder

ARIYARATNA

LOVE
ALSO IN MIND

If my love could talk
It would say much more than me
If my love could touch
It would embrace more than me
If my love could see
It would picture more than me
Just that my love could not…
Since you are not with me

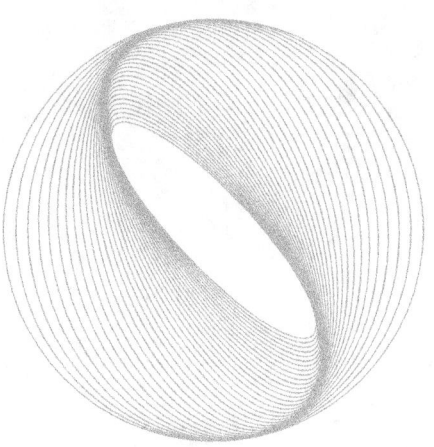

My Love

LOVE
ALSO IN MIND

I try to find a reason at times
To talk to you for a while
To see if I can this time define
Why my heart reaches out to find
Without being all numb and sad
You and I should be happy and glad
I guess I will wait for you to return
Some words of love to adjourn

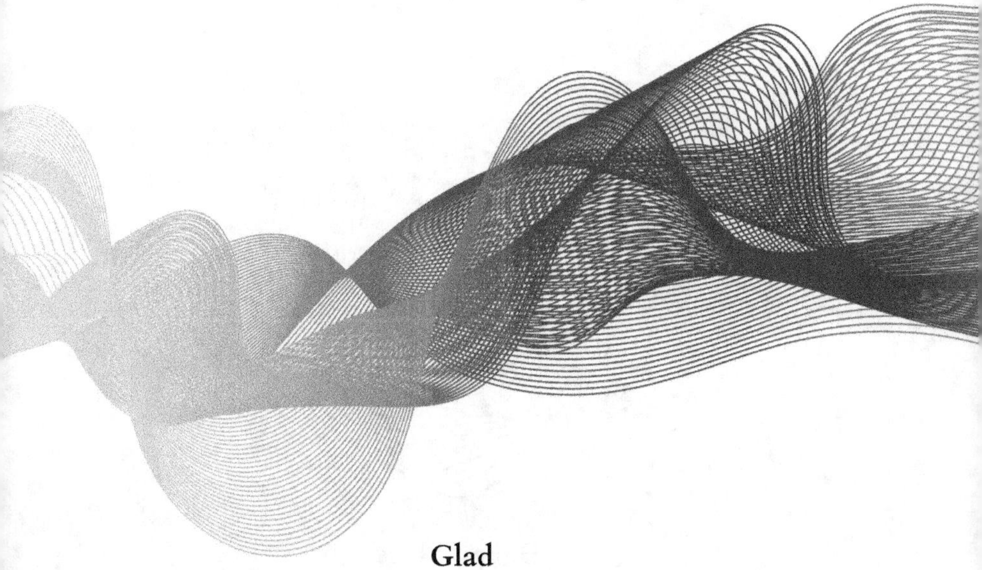

Glad

ARIYARATNA

LOVE
ALSO IN MIND

It takes a second to say
I love you
And a life time to show it,

But with you,
Every second is a life time,
Each life time where I'll love you

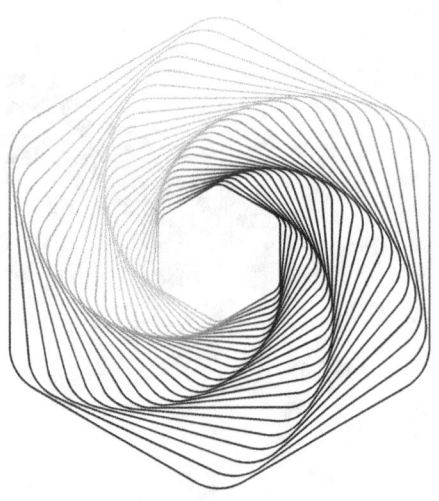

Happy Place

LOVE
ALSO IN MIND

Remember my broken heart
That I told you NOT to carefully fix
Well it's breaking again
Into much smaller pieces

And this time
You are NOT there, to NOT listen

NOT

ARIYARATNA

LOVE
ALSO IN MIND

Every night the Moon is there,
And every night it's not,
I will regret you not being here,
I would be truly Lost

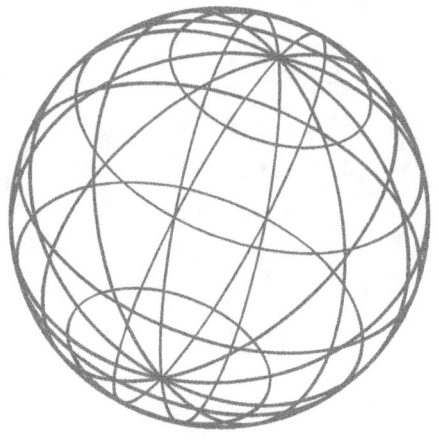

Regret

ARIYARATNA

LOVE
ALSO IN MIND

I tend to draw, I try to write
I work to make the world, Look nice
From each moonrise to sunset
From this island to its offset
What I could never believe
Is how good it looks watching you leave

That Arse

ARIYARATNA

LOVE
ALSO IN MIND

Forget the Moon, Shoot the Stars
End the Waves and keep the cars
Throw the Flowers, wash the Shine
Break the Magic, it's not Mine
Content and Blissful with no Drama
I think I'll leave meeting you, to Karma

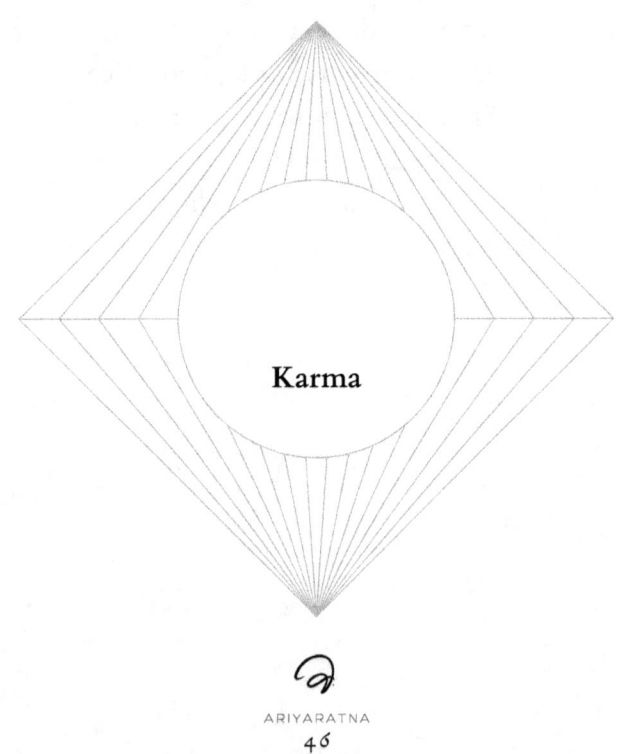

Karma

LOVE
ALSO IN MIND

I know for sure, I was meant to Love you
I just dont know, if I was meant to Stop

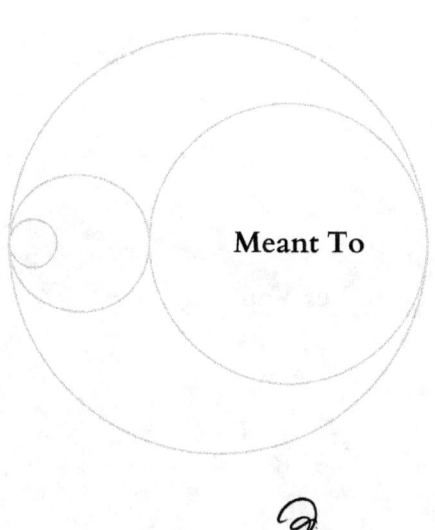

Meant To

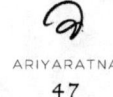

ARIYARATNA

LOVE
ALSO IN MIND

Let's clear your schedule
Tonight I am making plans with you

Yes You

LOVE
ALSO IN MIND

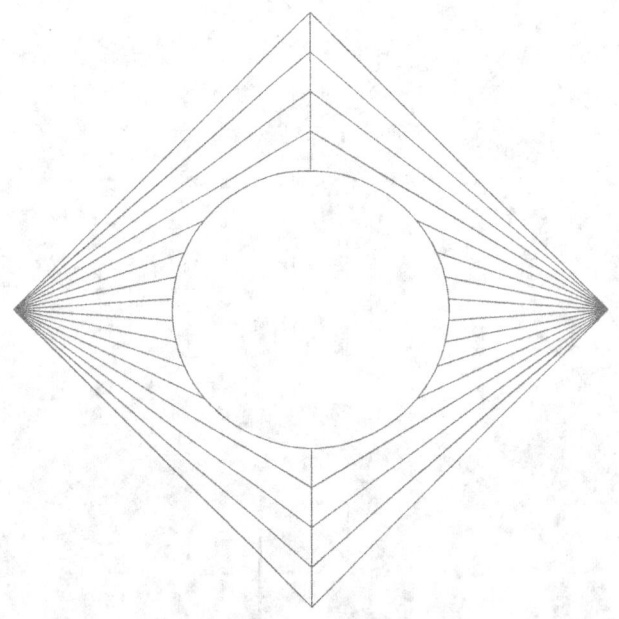

You made me love
Like I have never been hurt before

You

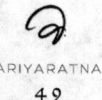

ARIYARATNA

ALSO IN MIND

CHAPTER
3

FOREVER

Forget Time

FOREVER
ALSO IN MIND

Wish List:
a Flying Unicorn
And
an Unbreakable Heart

Imagine-Ne-really

FOREVER
ALSO IN MIND

What I miss the most is ME

The ME when I am with YOU

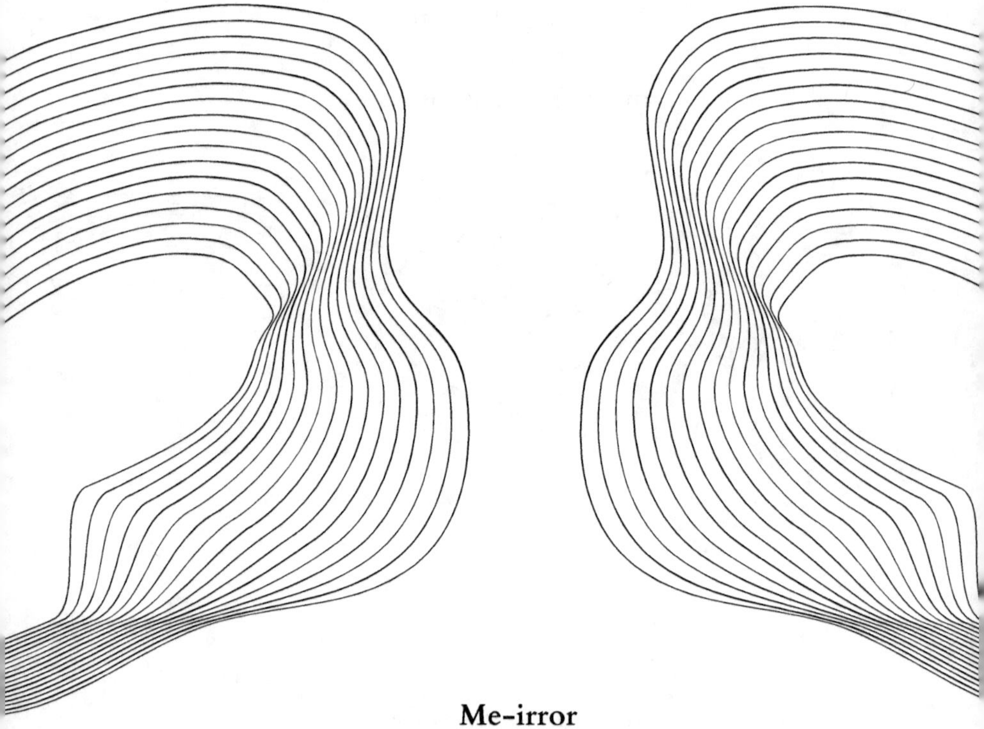

Me-irror

ARIYARATNA

FOREVER
ALSO IN MIND

I Miss Plastic Cups
And
Honest Hearts

Honest

ARIYARATNA

FOREVER
ALSO IN MIND

Full Moon
&
Empty heart

Moon

FOREVER
ALSO IN MIND

Blowing away to remove the flame
Of the candle, you lit in my Heart,
Forgetting my dragon's Breath
Although we are so so …so much
Apart

Dragons Breath

ARIYARATNA

FOREVER
ALSO IN MIND

I would burn like the sun for her
Sometimes a little too hot
Sometimes a little too bright
Sometimes not enough
Sometimes with all my might
But I would always Burn
Burn all day.. Burn all night

Burn

ARIYARATNA

I move with the wind
I hide with the clouds
I sleep with the dark
I avoid the crowds
I scuff off your mark
I know it's too soon
Too tired myself
Of Avoiding the moon

Avoid

FOREVER
ALSO IN MIND

Be chirpy
Be curious
Be funny
Be furious
Be Happy
Be Glad
Be anything you want
Just not Sad

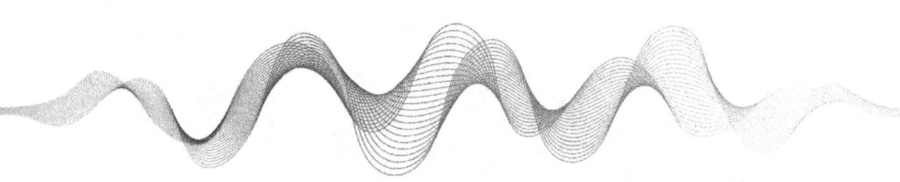

Be

ARIYARATNA

FOREVER
ALSO IN MIND

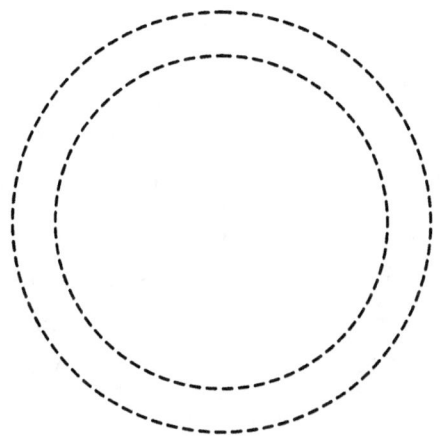

One thing you ask them to do
Is the One thing they don't do
And then you can't stop One-dering
Why they couldn't do

One

FOREVER
ALSO IN MIND

Where are you to warm my soul
Where are you to cushion my falls
Where are you to feed my hunger
Where are you to feel my thunder
Where are you to make my mind
Where are you to make me kind
Where are you to give my love

What you must be thinking is right above

Where are You?

FOREVER
ALSO IN MIND

Why don't you think about it
Why don't you see
What don't you like about it
What it could be
When you are here
When you are mine
How it makes me glad
How it makes me fine

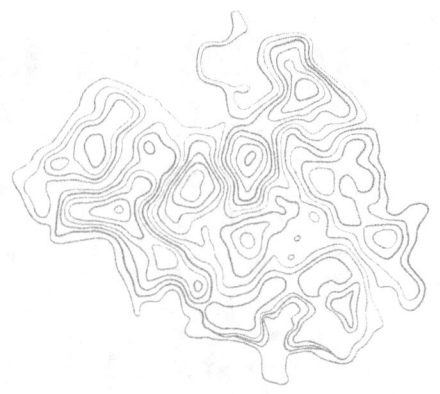

Where?

FOREVER
ALSO IN MIND

I think if you miss someone
You should say
If you want someone
You should stay
If you need someone
You should chase
If you love someone
give them space

Space

FOREVER
ALSO IN MIND

End this Gloom
To Fill my Room
With her Moonshine Smile

Simply You

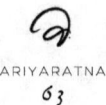
ARIYARATNA

FOREVER
ALSO IN MIND

You are Most brave either
When you have nothing to lose
Or
When you have everything to lose

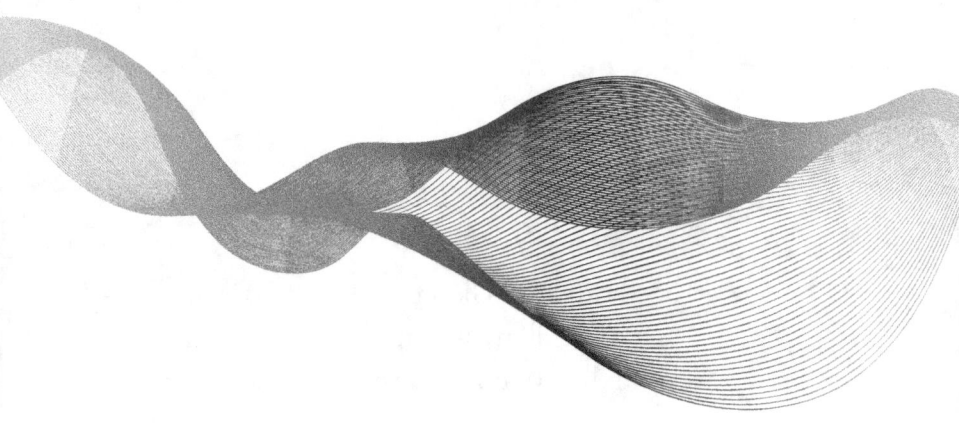

No Bravest

ARIYARATNA

FOREVER
ALSO IN MIND

Life is always exciting enough with glee,
Just need to look through the right glasses regularly,
Look hard for the colours and you will see,
only if you use your imagination, for all its glory.

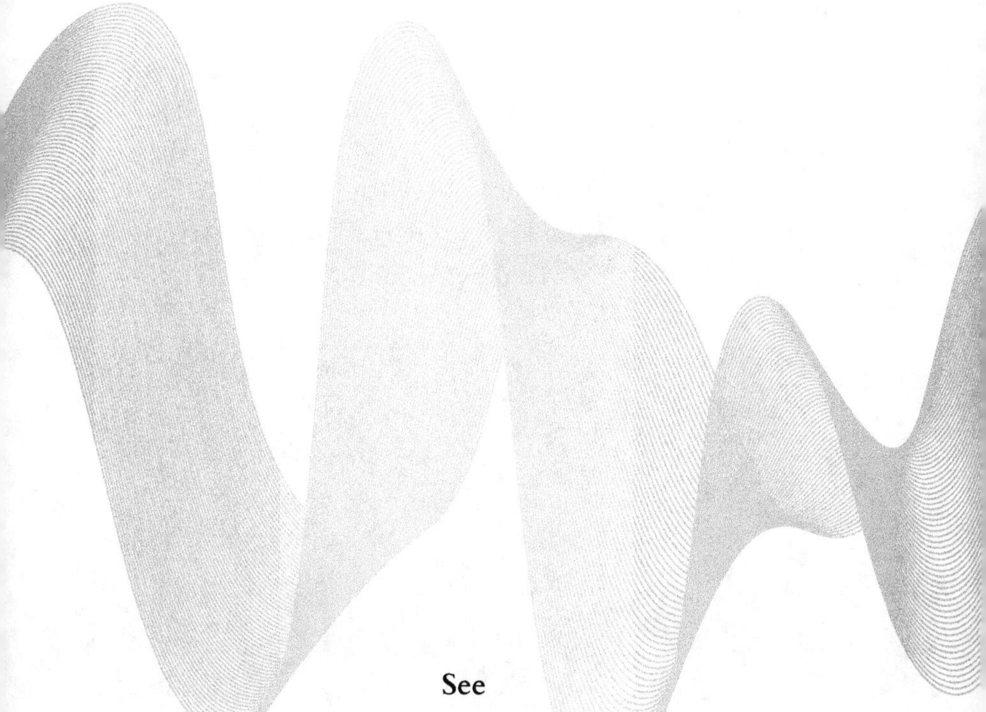

See

ARIYARATNA

FOREVER
ALSO IN MIND

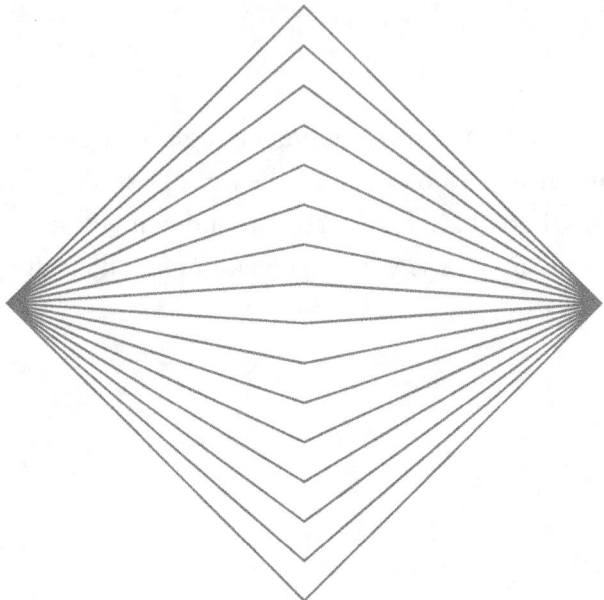

Away from Keyboard
No Feelings Record
Silent by Accord

AFK

ARIYARATNA

FOREVER
ALSO IN MIND

Mondays are my favorite
I almost Entirely Forget you
existed…
…….Almost

Favorite

FOREVER
ALSO IN MIND

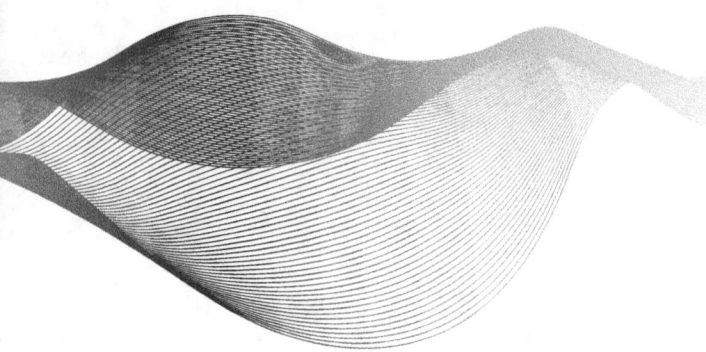

Escape with me
To my dreams
Where the plains
Meet the streams
And you are in my arms
Before my next Alarm

Hit Snooze

FOREVER
ALSO IN MIND

Even the Brave
Reconsider

Even

ARIYARATNA

FOREVER
ALSO IN MIND

Where are you? I want you now
Its late, tell me why and how
Amongst the Stars, beyond the clouds
After the moon, and behind the crowds
I love to play your games to miss
When will you lean to kiss

Rain

ARIYARATNA

ALSO IN MIND

CHAPTER
4

MORE

Becoming the Beyond

MORE
ALSO IN MIND

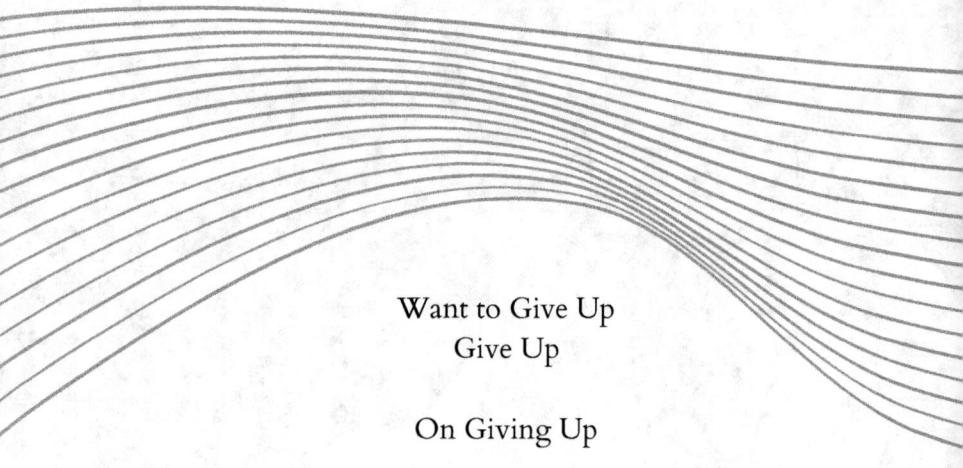

Want to Give Up
Give Up

On Giving Up

Giving

ARIYARATNA
72

MORE
ALSO IN MIND

This world is so so unfair
I wish I could live with the Moon
I'd be much happier there

Unfair

What you see of the Moon,
Is what she lets you,
Completely Incomplete at times,
Incompletely complete at times,

Just Like My Heart

Different Minds want you to believe
Different Classes want you to forgive
Different Dreams want you to chase
Different People want you to taste
Different Hopes want you to keep
Different Hearts want you… my sleep

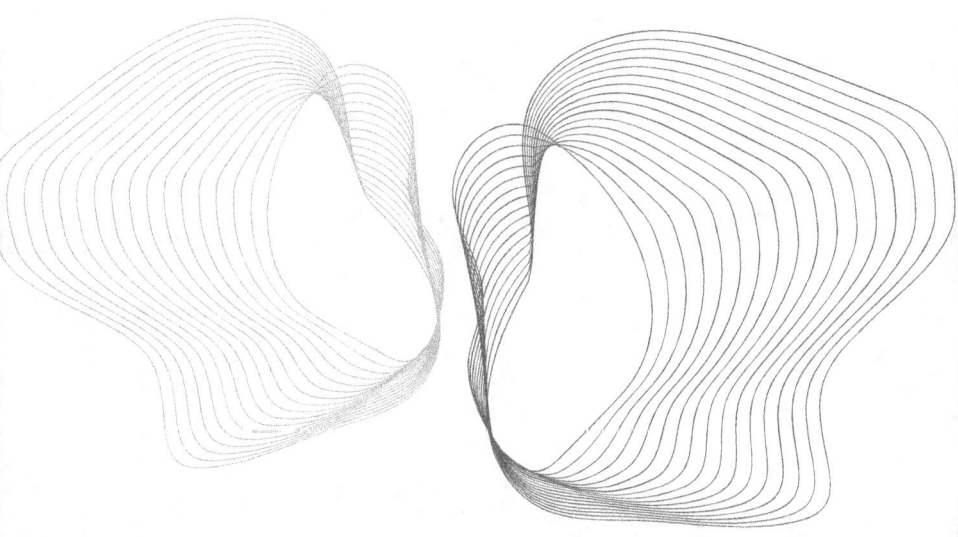

Different Discussion

MORE
ALSO IN MIND

No Matter you follow me or Not
No Matter you repost this or Not
No Matter you like this or Not
No Matter you share this or Not
No Matter you save this or Not
No Matter… the world still loves you a lot

Spread the world we all need it

No Matter

ARIYARATNA

Rains remind me
Of what I should forget
Lighting teases me
Of a what I do regret
Thunder scolds me
Of a why I would just let let
Winds blow away all that
With this Soul I met, not yet

May Weather

MORE
ALSO IN MIND

And then there are some nights
When you just want to loose

Just

ARIYARATNA

MORE
ALSO IN MIND

Double Bed
Single Me
Zero You
Minus US

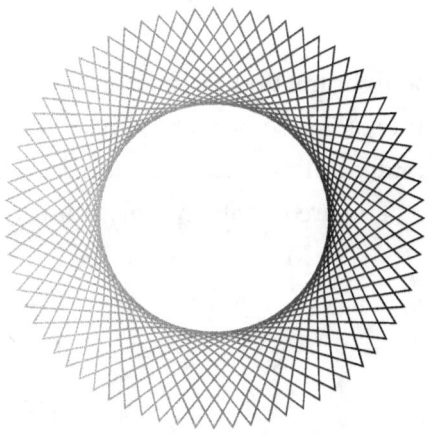

Count

MORE
ALSO IN MIND

You light me up like the northern skies
With colours so pure, both near and far.
Without you I'm in the dark for many miles
You are my always, my muse,
My only Aurora

Aurora

ARIYARATNA

MORE
ALSO IN MIND

Omg how can I not remember
To write something about November
Did it just sneak up on us all
Making me miss, my favorite Season: Fall

Noticing November

MORE
ALSO IN MIND

We are More afraid
Of
Reality checks
than
Security checks

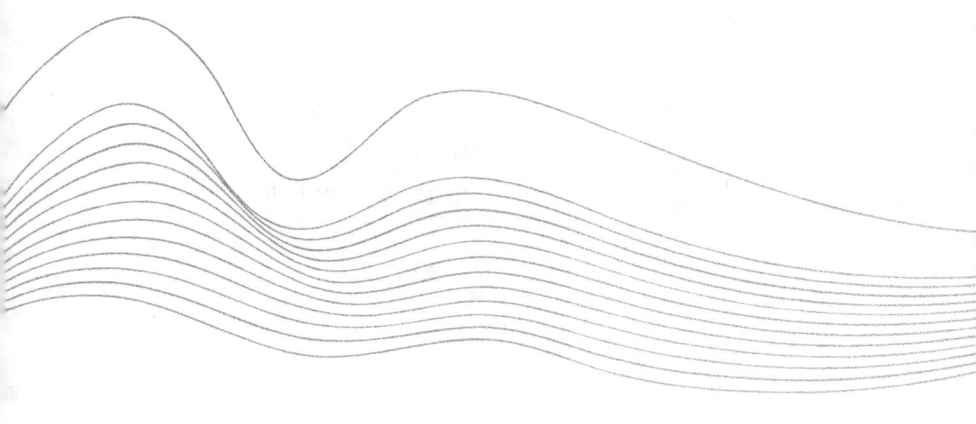

Checks

ARIYARATNA

MORE
ALSO IN MIND

Silence Incarnate

Quiet

ARIYARATNA

MORE
ALSO IN MIND

Are you as excited as I am
to see the Moon,
I can't believe it's already June

Jealous June

MORE
ALSO IN MIND

I miss the moon during the night,
During the day,
I miss the fondle, the fight,
in every different way,
I miss what's right,
I wish it's not June and it's May

Miss Moon May

MORE
ALSO IN MIND

Wait hold on,
What are you doing?
Isn't this how you,
Start trouble brewing?
Haven't you learnt,
Enough to know
That some hearts
Have love just for Show

For Show for Sure

MORE
ALSO IN MIND

I was happy and alone, I was rarely on my phone
Only to find, You intruding my mind
Days to weeks, You polluted this freak
With desires and futures, then With more excuses
It took me a while to get back on my horse
I'm fine, I'm good with no remorse
I feel like I've had enough and more battles
Moving on strong, might move to Seattle

Intrude & Pollute

ARIYARATNA

MORE
ALSO IN MIND

Blue like the sapphire? Or Blue like the sky?
Blue like the Nile? Or Blue like the dye?
Blue like the ticks? Or Blue like the nights?
Blue like the Aurora? Or Blue like the lights?
Blue like the sea? Or Blue like the hills?
Blue like my heart? Or Blue like these pills?

When you Say Blue

ARIYARATNA

MORE
ALSO IN MIND

Peace so Fable
My Soul Cradle

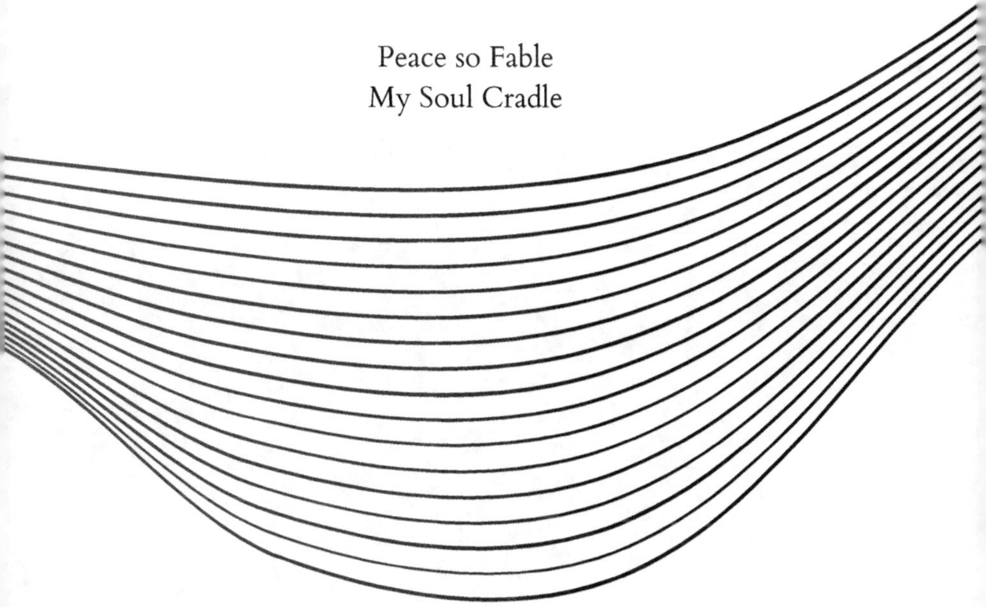

Soul Cradle

ARIYARATNA
89

MORE
ALSO IN MIND

Next time I will find you over fires burning
Next time I will find you over the waves roaring
Next time I will find you before anyone
Next time I will find you, this time..
This time my time is almost done.

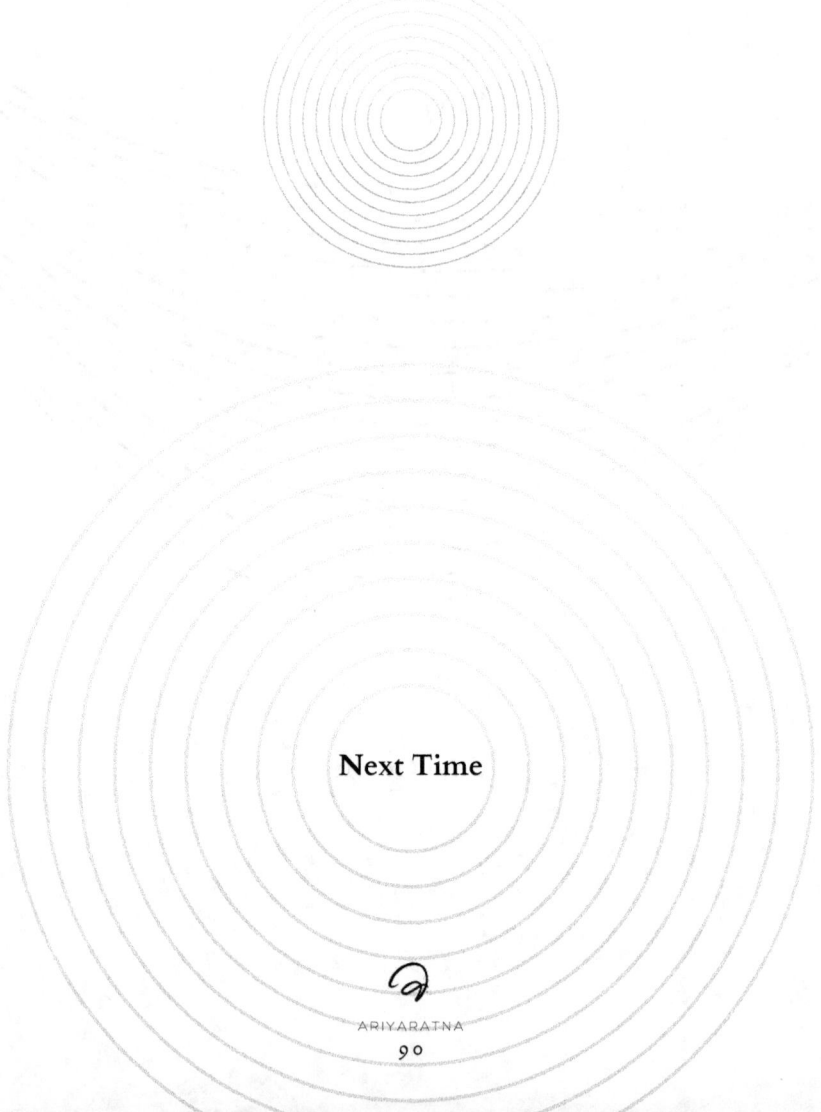

Next Time

ALSO IN MIND

LEFT BLANK FOR YOUR OWN POEM ON
RECREATE

ALSO IN MIND

LEFT BLANK FOR YOUR OWN POEM ON
LOVE

LEFT BLANK FOR YOUR OWN POEM ON
FOREVER

LEFT BLANK FOR YOUR OWN POEM ON MORE

THANK YOU

ALSO IN MIND

ABOUT THE AUTHOR

Chanaka Ariyaratna is a Sri Lankan artist, poet, architect, and writer based in Australia. He has been writing poetry since he was a teenager and holds a true passion for the art form. His poetry explores themes of identity, creation, love, and spirituality and is known for its unique style that blends Eastern and Western influences.

A true believer of the power of creative expression, Chanaka is also an artist favouring mixed media. Carefree and whimsical but embodied with intricate detail and heavy emotion, Ariyaratna's artwork is often described as a paradox of artistic expression.

A poet and artist by nature and a prolific architect by design, Chanaka has been creating architecture for over 16 years. Ariyaratna's architecture is known for its innovative design and incorporation of front-line technology. He emphasizes spatial themes and a progressive approach to design.

When he's not creating, Chanaka enjoys spending time with his loved ones and exploring the world around him. He hopes to continue sharing his creative vision with the world, be it through poetry, art or architecture design.

www.ingramcontent.com/pod-product-compliance
Lightning Source LLC
Chambersburg PA
CBHW070310010526
44107CB00056B/2551